SPOTLIGHT ON
AN EQUITABLE WORLD

T0284463

BECOMING AN ACTIVE CITIZEN

Mary Ratzer

ROSEN
PUBLISHING

Published in 2025 by The Rosen Publishing Group, Inc.
2544 Clinton Street, Buffalo, NY 14224

Copyright © 2025 by The Rosen Publishing Group, Inc.

First Edition

All rights reserved. No part of this book may be reproduced in any form without permission in writing from the publisher, except by a reviewer.

Editor: Greg Roza
Book Design: Michael Flynn

Photo Credits: Cover Photoroyalty/Shutterstock.com; cover, p. 3 (hands) Dedraw Studio/Shutterstock.com; (series Earth icon) v4ndhira/Shutterstock.com; p. 5 Olenka2104/Shutterstock.com; p. 6 goodluz/Shutterstock.com; p. 7 Monkey Business Images/Shutterstock.com; p. 8 Stephen Coburn/Shutterstock.com; p. 9 AnnaBabich/Shutterstock.com; p. 10 Tommy Alven/Shutterstock.com; p. 11 https://commons.wikimedia.org/wiki/File:Ehsan_Ullah_Khan_meets_a_shy_and_afraid_Iqbal_Masih.png; p. 13 https://commons.wikimedia.org/wiki/File:Albany_Medical_Center.jpg; p. 14 Ulianenko Dmitrii/Shutterstock.com; p. 15 Pipas Imagery/Shutterstock.com; p. 17 i_am_zews/Shutterstock.com; p. 18 Media Lens King/Shutterstock.com; p. 19 T. Schneider/Shutterstock.com; p. 21 K M H P H O T O V I D E O/Shutterstock.com; p. 22 Everett Collection Historical/Alamy Stock Photo; p. 23 https://commons.wikimedia.org/wiki/File:Martin_Luther_King_Jr._addresses_a_crowd_from_the_steps_of_the_Lincoln_Memorial,_USMC-09611.jpg; p. 25 https://commons.wikimedia.org/wiki/File:Exhibit_on_Freedom_Riders_-_Center_for_Civil_and_Human_Rights_-_Atlanta_-_Georgia_-_USA_(33468216774).jpg; p. 26 Everett Collection/Shutterstock.com; p. 27 courtesy of the Library of Congress; p. 29 Jon Chica/Shutterstock.com.

Library of Congress Cataloging-in-Publication Data

Names: Ratzer, Mary Boyd, author.
Title: Becoming an active citizen / Mary Ratzer.
Description: Buffalo : Rosen Publishing, [2025] | Series: Spotlight on an
    equitable world. | Includes index.
Identifiers: LCCN 2023055904 (print) | LCCN 2023055905 (ebook) | ISBN
    9781499477269 (library binding) | ISBN 9781499477382 (paperback) | ISBN
    9781499476989 (ebook)
Subjects: LCSH: Political participation--Juvenile literature. |
    Citizenship--Juvenile literature. | Community life--Juvenile literature.
    | Youth--Political activity--Juvenile literature.
Classification: LCC JF799 .R36 2025 (print) | LCC JF799 (ebook) | DDC
    323/.042--dc23/eng/20240110
LC record available at https://lccn.loc.gov/2023055904
LC ebook record available at https://lccn.loc.gov/2023055905

Manufactured in the United States of America

Some of the images in this book illustrate individuals who are models. The depictions do not imply actual situations or events.

CPSIA Compliance Information: Batch #CSRYA25. For further information contact Rosen Publishing at 1-800-237-9932.

Find us on

CONTENTS

Chapter One

MIRRORS AND WINDOWS

You are a citizen. You belong to a community, a nation, a world. When you grow into the role of active citizen you can look into a mirror. What do you see as a citizen who has decided to be a part of finding solutions? Do you see your values reflected in your actions? Do you hear your beliefs in your words? Do you see where your awareness led you? Does the mirror reflect that you care about a positive change?

Active citizens work with others and make their communities better. When you are an active citizen, your world grows bigger. You might become aware of unfairness in your community. Becoming aware, you open a window to your real world and problems that need to be solved. Perhaps you open a window by understanding how attitudes could have hurtful consequences. Understanding opens a window into another person's experience and feelings. Reading about or listening to others are windows to a world that needs you as an active citizen and a part of the solutions.

Activism can happen with just one person speaking up when unfairness or bias affects someone. A single voice with a heartfelt message for human dignity may change the minds of just a few others, but still change minds. A small group of people with a goal to stop injustice can change the lives of many. Young activists understand the problems in one school or one neighborhood and do something to help. Communities are better places to be when all the little acts for fairness come together.

Becoming an active citizen requires that you really get to know yourself and understand how your beliefs shape the person you are.

Chapter Two

STUDENTS AND CIVIC ACTION

Across America, social studies teachers prepare learners to participate in their communities and act as citizens in order to solve problems. This is called civic action, and it is the peak of preparation for living in a democratic society. This quote from educational leaders is meant for teachers, but see if it makes sense for you:

"Now more than ever, students need the . . . power to recognize societal problems; ask good questions and develop . . . investigations into them; consider possible solutions and consequences; separate evidence . . . from opinions; and communicate and act upon what they learn."

Are there any issues in your school that you think need to be addressed? The first step is to talk to others and research the issue to figure out what could be done to fix it.

Tackling school and community issues needs preparation and new skills. What it takes to be ready for active citizenship is unique to each student. Their experience, personal ideas, current needs, and future goals count. Schools engage learners in opportunities to learn and grow into active citizens. Learning to recognize problems in the community is an important step. The search for causes and effects of a problem leads to awareness and experience.

Asking good questions to understand the problem is a key part of investigating issues. When you are informed and ready to take action, you can work on a plan. Possible solutions and consequences of those solutions require creative and informed thinking. Once you launch your plan for action, gather evidence of the plan's success or the need to revise it. Reflecting and evaluating will guide you through each new problem.

Chapter Three

WANT AD FOR ACTIVE CITIZENS

The National Council for Social Studies and education departments across the country are recognizing the need for middle school and high school students to participate as active citizens. As agents of positive change, diverse student voices draw on their experiences and perspectives.

Your school may be awarding the Seal of Civic Readiness to students. This accomplishment is based on demonstrating respect for the rights of others, identifying situations that require social actions, and demonstrating knowledge, responsibility, values, and community engagement. Civic readiness is the ability to make a positive difference in the public life of communities through a combination of civic knowledge, skills, actions, and experiences.

WANTED

Active citizens who can work for fairness, social justice, and equity in this community. Opportunities available. Experience welcome but not required.

SKILLS AND ATTITUDES NEEDED

- Care about the well-being of others and motivation to be a part of positive change
- Awareness of problems with fairness and justice
- Problem-solving skills including identifying causes and consequences
- Investigation and research skills, reading for information
- Being an ally, speaking up and supporting others
- Curiosity and open-mindedness about human needs and rights
- Ability to collaborate and work as part of a team
- Time management and responsibility for tasks
- Relationship skills, active listening, conflict resolution
- Communication that works for different audiences
- Ability to share ideas and information in speech and writing
- Respect for cultures and differences
- Action planning with a team
- Determination, resilience, confidence, self-awareness
- Planning and evaluating results of projects and refining them
- Potential to learn leadership skills

Does this "want ad" speak to you? Do you think you have what it takes to become an active citizen?

Chapter Four

BEING A PART OF THE SOLUTION

Many young people live in a culture that values self-interest and personal gain. Turning instead to action for the well-being of others is a leap toward civic responsibility. Recognizing stepping up as the right thing to do is very important in the growth of values and identity. Accomplishing this by engaging with others who share a sense of purpose brings personal rewards.

Role models could be as familiar as teachers, parents, or peers sitting next to you on the bus. An example from 2023 is the account of a seventh grader who jumped into action when the driver of his school bus lost consciousness. Seventh grader Dillon, from the Warren School District in Michigan, did not hesitate to take over and steer the bus to safety, telling his peers to call 911. He has been commended for his quick action.

Masih was just 12 years old when he died. However, he influenced and inspired many people to follow his lead as an active citizen. He is remembered as a hero to many.

The students at Broad Meadows Middle School in Quincy, Massachusetts, met Iqbal Masih when he came to their school as a winner of a youth action award. Iqbal was sold into child labor at age five in Pakistan, chained to a loom and working around 14 hours a day. He contacted an organization that frees children in Pakistan from child labor and became an advocate for his fellow workers and fought successfully against child labor. He attended a school created for child laborers by a labor organization. Sharing the message that child labor was illegal, he persuaded many to seek freedom and go to school. Students in Quincy launched a national funding campaign to build a school in Pakistan using the internet and their creativity.

Chapter Five

HANNAH'S HIDEAWAY

The Melodies Center for Childhood Cancer and Blood Disorders is in Albany, New York. Albany Medical Center treats seriously ill kids in a typical hospital setting. Nurses dash in and out of rooms, machines beep, and young people fight to survive with long hours and days of treatments. Visiting families wait, support, and worry.

A young leukemia patient, Hannah Priamo, had a creative idea to make the hospital a more comforting and warmer place for kids and their families. Hannah stood out at the medical center for her positive attitude and grace in handling treatment. Laughter could be heard in spaces where Hannah was receiving care. Her father, Paul Priamo, shared Hannah's favorite quote from John F. Kennedy: "One person can make a difference, and everyone should try."

So Hannah became an active citizen for patients and their families, planning to set up a kitchen space in the center. Families and patients could find comfort in a homelike haven. Coffee and snacks could help to ease hours of waiting and stress.

Brainstorming with hospital staff, Hannah came up with a Melodies Family Feud Fundraiser with doctors competing with nurses. Sadly, Hannah died a month before the fundraiser, but others picked up the plan. The hospital built Hannah's dream kitchen with a successful fundraising effort, earning $18,000. Community businesses contributed to renovations and friends of Hannah's family donated money to buy furniture and food to stock the kitchen. Hannah made a difference that started with empathy and an idea.

Construction of Hannah's Hideaway was paused during the COVID-19 pandemic. It was completed in 2022.

Chapter Six

ACTIVE CITIZENS START WITH AN IDEA

Creativity is a powerful skill for young active citizens. Creative ideas lead to solutions. When adolescents find allies and tap into the energy of a team, they excel at coming up with great ideas.

West Branch, Iowa—Seventh graders in West Branch Middle School launched a project to remove used oil filters from landfills. The used filters leak oil into land and water, causing environmental problems. After collecting them and removing the oil from them, the students then properly disposed of the oil and recycled the metal in the filters. They are trying to make discarding used oil filters illegal in their state. Their school participates in the Leader in Me program that emphasizes creativity and collaboration.

The students in West Branch identified a problem in their community and collaborated with one another to make a positive change. It's not always easy, but as a team, we can make our communities a safer place to live.

East Providence, Rhode Island—East Providence is a city where about half of the students and families could benefit from programs that ensure food security. Using the Community School Model, a food pantry has been set up in schools there with fresh produce along with healthy food choices. A local partnership of citizens included the Shop & Stop grocery chain, the We Share Hope community agency, school leaders, and local students in East Providence High School.

State of Illinois—A sharp rise in Asian American hate crimes inspired the State of Illinois to put into law the TEAACH Act to ensure that the next generation of students learn about Asian American heritage. A lack of knowledge can lead to discrimination. Youth opinion pieces in newspapers added to this advocacy effort.

Chapter Seven

ADVANTAGES AND DISADVANTAGES

Advantages and disadvantages affect human needs and human rights. Studies show that inequity in communities affects community members' access to nutrition, healthcare, education, and shelter. How can solutions help disadvantaged members of a community get what they need to thrive? This is the purpose of social justice and working for equity. Think about these facts that tell a story of inequity for kids:

- State funding for education varies across America, leading to differences in opportunities and success for kids.

- While one state invests more than $24,000 a year in each student's education, another spends about $7,600 per student.

- Many countries provide equitable funding for all schools through their governments. Some of these countries have the most successful learners in the world.

- Some schools are in areas where many families earn lower incomes than neighboring areas. This affects the resources available for learners and the quality of teachers.

- Schools in low-income areas offer fewer upper-level math and science courses that are needed for success in college.

- Students in low-income areas have disadvantages with technology, digital tools, and access to internet connections.

NO TO POVERTY

Why is equity important for all U.S. citizens? Is it fair that some struggle more than others to get by? What can be done to help?

- One in seven kids under the age of 18 lives in poverty in America.

- Younger children are more likely to live in poverty than older children.

- America has one of the highest rates of child poverty despite having a very high rate of wealth.

- Children living in poverty are more likely to have health problems because of the lack of clean air, clean water, shelter, and good nutrition.

- Children of color are nearly three times more likely to experience poverty than white children.

BENEFITS AND BURDENS

Social justice activists see the community as a place where some receive the benefits of society, and some receive the burdens. Your community might have benefits such as safe neighborhoods and clean air. Your community might have burdens such as hunger or barriers to healthcare for all. Communities provide and protect the resources that citizens need to live a good life. Injustice happens when those needs to live a good life are met for some and not for others. Some citizens have benefits. Some have burdens.

Doctors Without Borders is a charitable organization. It provides healthcare to people in areas affected by war, sickness, and poverty.

MEDECINS SANS FRONTIERES
DOCTORS WITHOUT BORDERS

Action for social justice has the goal of fairness. Activists shine a light on where and how some citizens are not thriving. They work to change the minds of those who are not aware or do not care about equity. They communicate with leaders and decision-makers to make them understand problems. Activists investigate and use evidence to start the climb to solutions. Activists seek allies and strengthen their effort for positive change.

Activism is at work wherever there are communities. The entire world is a community of diverse human beings. Some activists make the choice to solve a problem that is worldwide. Widespread efforts by the United Nations, large organizations like Doctors Without Borders, and international agencies use the contributions from millions of people to fund their activism across the world.

Time, talent, money, resources, and people come together to end poverty, educate those without schools, and support refugees. Sometimes activists work to solve big problems like racism or unequal human rights in just one country or just one city. The energy and determination of many activists make change happen.

Chapter Nine

THE TIPPING POINT

Timing is everything. This can be true in advocacy and civic action. Problems have a beginning and hopefully an end. Be aware of the people affected by the problem and the ways they are impacted by it. Sometimes the time for action comes quickly. If basic human needs, such as health, well-being, and safety are at risk, then that may be the tipping point.

Sometimes problems progress slowly, over many years, before a tipping point for action is reached. Trust your feelings and empathy to know when to act. Also consider that solutions can take time.

Youth have joined together in large numbers to declare in words and actions that now is the time to act. Some of the strongest voices discussing climate change are those of young people who will inherit a planet in crisis. As school violence also continues to put young lives at risk, the students at Marjory Stoneman Douglas High School have spoken clearly to the entire nation saying that this must stop. Their voices have been joined by millions of others who say that there needs to be an end to school shootings in the United States.

Young people in America have joined together before and made the entire nation wake up to a problem. Protesting the War in Vietnam (1954–1975) involved millions of students willing to take action despite consequences. Students who never saw themselves as leaders grew up to be leaders. Decide to be a part of solutions when a moment arises that touches your sense of justice.

Marjory Stoneman Douglas High School in Parkland, Florida, experienced a mass shooting on February 14, 2018, that resulted in the death of 17 students. This photograph shows students protesting lax gun laws just days after the shooting.

Chapter Ten

YOUNG ACTIVISTS AND CIVIL RIGHTS

In the 1960s, the Civil Rights Movement drew children, teenagers, and young adults into roles as active citizens. A generation of young people made the decision to fight for civil rights. Joining adults in meetings, marches, violence, and imprisonment, they took risks to end segregation, racism, and mistreatment. Joyce Ladner, author and civil rights activist, reflected on why she became an active part of this struggle: "The movement was the most exciting thing that one could engage in … I said that there was no more exciting time." Her uncle told her: "Your generation is going to change things."

In 1963 in Birmingham, Alabama, more than 5,000 students organized a march to the mayor's office to discuss segregation. Police used water hoses and police dogs to chase off the protestors.

Martin Luther King Jr. is a famous Civil Rights Movement leader and activist. His work changed the lives of millions of Black Americans.

Several activists interviewed for the Civil Rights History Project were in elementary school when they joined the movement. When he was only 12, Freeman Hrabowski was inspired to march in the Birmingham Children's Crusade of 1963. While sitting in the back of church one Sunday, his ears perked up when he heard a man speak about a march for integrated schools. Schools were still unequal and segregated by race, which was against federal law. Hrabowski was arrested at the march and spent many days in prison. However, photographs of police and dogs attacking the children soon drew nationwide attention. Hrabowski remembers that at the prison, Dr. Martin Luther King Jr. told him and the other children, "What you do this day will have an impact on children yet unborn." Hrabowski later recalled: "I'll never forget that. I didn't even understand it, but I knew it was powerful, powerful, very powerful."

Chapter Eleven

FREEDOM AND EQUAL RIGHTS

Think about graduating from high school and starting college in 1961. The Civil Rights Movement worked to end discrimination so all citizens in America had the same rights. Travel for Black people involved segregation, loss of dignity, and punishment for breaking racist rules. Bus terminals had segregated areas that were strictly enforced. Water fountains, bathrooms, food counters, restaurant seating, boarding areas, and entrances and exits were divided for white people and Black people. Seating on buses had racist restrictions. Blacks sat away from whites in the back of buses. The Supreme Court banned all of this unfairness, but it stayed in place. As an 18 year old, and an active citizen, you might have decided to refuse to cooperate with racism and become a Freedom Rider.

Young college students, including the late senator from North Carolina, John Lewis, became Freedom Riders. Young men and women, Black and white, traveled by bus through the South in their best clothes, housed by supporters, and purposely tried to break the racist rules. Black people tried to sit with white people, sat in the front of the bus, drank from whites-only water fountains, and used reserved spaces freely. Threatened, beaten, arrested, trapped in a bus set on fire, attacked, and put on trial, they risked safety and even their lives. Over time, 436 Freedom Riders succeeded in advocating freedom and dignity for Black people.

Shown here are the mugshots of Freedom Riders who were arrested for breaking racist laws in Jackson, Mississippi.

Chapter Twelve

HISTORIC ACTIVE CITIZENSHIP AND CHILD LABOR

From 1860 to 1920, child labor in America was common. Because children earned less than adults, employers made more profits by hiring children. They worked at dangerous jobs six days a week, for at least 10 hours a day. Young workers spent long hours with dangerous machines and unsafe air in textile mills and glass factories. They also worked as farm laborers.

Over 100 years ago, some young people sold newspapers to support themselves and their families. Coming from poor immigrant families, they were called newsies. They sold papers on city streets for one cent. At the end of the evening, if they sold 100 papers, they

This photograph from 1908 shows a group of newspaper boys in New York City preparing to sell the morning paper. Newsboys, or newsies, worked long hours for little pay.

Today in the United States, there are laws in place to prevent companies from taking advantage of child labor.

made 50 cents. If they sold less than 50, they lost money. In 1889, the newsies went on strike. They organized and refused to sell papers when the price of papers went up. The action of newsies resulted in more fairness from the publishers.

Jobs like those in coal mines frequently caused adolescents and children to be injured or killed because of hazardous equipment. Coal dust and unsafe air quality caused suffering. Young miners went to work in the dark and came out of the mine in the dark. Parents in poverty lied about their children's ages to get them employed in mines.

In 1904, activists founded the National Child Labor Committee (NCLC). To raise awareness of the abuses of child labor, the NCLC hired sociologist Lewis Hine to photograph children working in fields, factories, mines, and city streets. His photos and reports raised public awareness. Congress was inspired by his evidence and passed national child labor legislation.

Chapter Thirteen

SOCIAL RESPONSIBILITY AND ACTION

Social responsibility is a very big idea. Making responsible decisions is the first step—decisions that are good for your well-being and the good of the community. Practice makes this a part of how you think. Paying attention to perspectives, solutions to problems, and consequences of actions is important. Making caring choices in your interactions with others is the basis of social responsibility. Opportunities to be a part of solving problems and making positive change result from social responsibility.

How does this work in your real world? Observe how socially responsible people around you think and act. Consider this example and others you may encounter.

A basketball coach lives in a city with street crime and frequent problems for kids after school. His goal is to mentor young boys, keep them out of gangs, and guide them in setting goals for their future. To do this, he needs to offer a fun time with basketball in a local park. Working with city resources, he gets the park cleaned up and basketball courts restored. As a coach, he persuades his friends in area schools to encourage kids to take part in games after school. Many show up. Funding equipment, snacks, T-shirts, and even sneakers, this active citizen becomes a friend and mentor to his players. He changes the path of many with his relationships and willingness to share.

What made this coach socially responsible? He worked for the common good. He made choices to benefit others. He knew problems needed to be solved. He made decisions that resulted in positive outcomes.

Selflessly helping the community is what it takes to become an active, caring citizen.

Chapter Fourteen

STANDING UP FOR RIGHTS

Standing up for the rights of others is the engine for social justice. Allies take the side of a person or group and add their voices or actions to the effort for change. This is happening right now all over the world. Global efforts of the United Nations protect and restore human rights. International responses to people in war zones and people facing famine fill the day's news. In small towns fighting for clean air, allies are at work. Celebrities like Billie Eilish, Beyoncé, and Damar Hamlin see the needs of others and invest in solutions. And the one person speaking up for fairness or someone's rights could be you.

The train derailments and resulting toxic pollution in East Palestine, Ohio, got the attention of government, environmental experts, and on-the-ground support. Natural disasters call on responses from volunteers and every possible resource. Louisiana's toxic air pollution affecting low-income neighborhoods and schools calls on local citizens to communicate and fight for solutions. Taking on corporations that release toxins into the air at their factories requires the strength of many voices. Silence does not make change. Active citizens make change.

Around the world, people are empowered when others speak up with them. Activists empathize with those who have lost rights and join their calls for justice. Advocates speak, write, and show up to communicate the problem. By visiting officials, engaging the media, writing letters, and making the problem visible, advocates work for lasting solutions.

GLOSSARY

activism: Using or supporting strong actions to help make changes in politics or society.

advocacy: The process or act of supporting a cause.

ally: One of two or more people or groups who work together.

bias: To have an unfair preference or dislike of something.

collaborate: To work together with others, often on an intellectual project.

discrimination: Unfairly treating people unequally because of their thoughts or beliefs.

empathy: The action of being aware of, comprehending, and being sensitive to another's experiences, thoughts, and feelings; also, the ability to share another's emotions.

equity: Fairness or justice in dealings between persons.

legislation: The action of making laws, or the laws themselves.

leukemia: A kind of cancer in which there is an abnormal increase in the number of white blood cells in the tissues and often in the blood.

mentor: Someone who teaches, gives guidance, or gives advice to someone, especially a less experienced person.

perspective: Point of view.

refugee: A migrant person who flees their homeland to escape disaster, persecution, or war.

renovation: To make like new again, or to put in good condition.

segregation: The separation of people based on race, class, sex, gender, or ethnicity.

sociologist: Someone trained in the science of social relationships, institutions, and society.

INDEX